Dedication

To Chiara, Landon, and Melanie

Acknowledgement

Writing this book has been something I've wanted to complete for quite some time. Seeing it come together has been a rewarding experience, and I am so grateful for the opportunity to share my words of encouragement for our children. I want to thank my husband, Ryan, for believing in me and helping me to pursue my dreams of completing my first book. He has been so supportive throughout this whole process, and I can't begin to describe how appreciative I am for him. I want to thank my children for the inspiration to write this book and hope that they know how amazing they are. I want to thank my parents, Greg and Carol, and my sister, Lauryn, for their words of encouragement and the confidence they gave me to follow my dreams and complete this book. Lastly, I want to thank my team at NY Book Publishers for taking my vision and creating it into the book you are holding today. Their hard work made this dream I had a reality.

About the Author

Katie Buchler is a dedicated wife and mother of three young children. Inspired by her desire to offer something meaningful to her kids and readers, she embarked on a journey to become an author. Her goal is to create engaging and educational books that instill confidence and positivity in children. Despite her busy life as a full-time mother, Katie finds time to indulge in her passions for baking, birdwatching, photography, and reading.

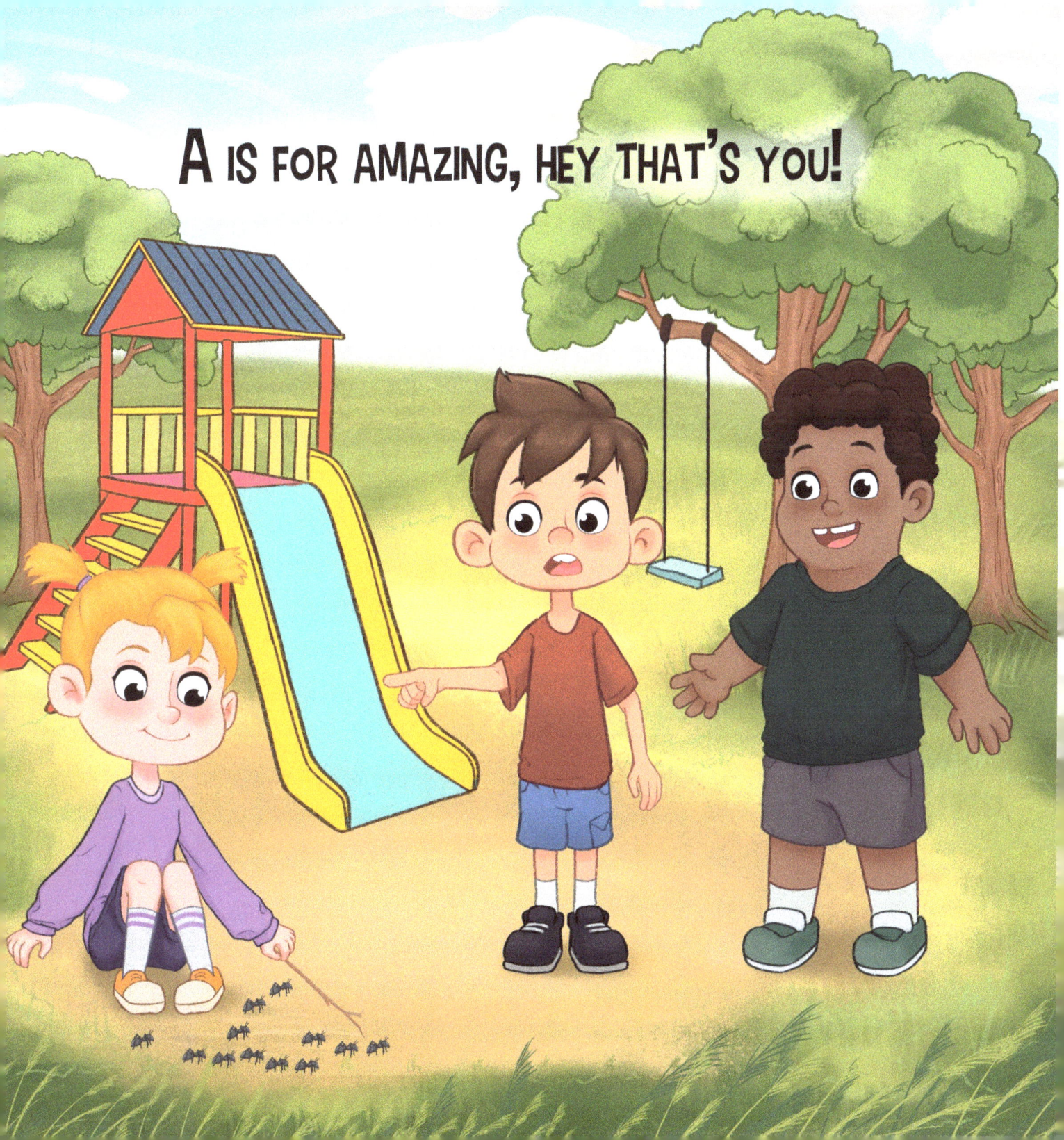

A IS FOR AMAZING, HEY THAT'S YOU!

B IS FOR BRAVE, IT'S TOUGH TO DO WHAT YOU DO!

C IS FOR CREATIVE, IN YOUR WORK AND PLAY!

D IS FOR DAZZLING, IN EACH AND EVERY WAY!

E IS FOR EXCITED, IN SPENDING TIME TOGETHER!

F IS FOR FUN, WHICH WE HAVE IN ANY WEATHER!

G IS FOR GREAT, JUST ONE WAY
TO DESCRIBE HOW SPECIAL YOU ARE!

H IS FOR HAPPY, YOUR SMILE IS THE BEST BY FAR!

I IS FOR INTELLIGENT, YOU ARE SO VERY SMART!

J IS FOR JOY, YOUR LAUGH IS JUST THE START!

K IS FOR KIND, YOU'RE THE BEST OF THE BUNCH!

L IS FOR LOVE, I LOVE YOU OH SO MUCH!

M IS FOR MAGNIFICENT, I AM SO IMPRESSED BY ALL THAT YOU DO!

N IS FOR NICE, THAT'S WHY EVERYONE WILL PLAY GAMES WITH YOU!

O IS FOR OUTSTANDING, WITH HOW YOU ARE AT EVERYTHING!

P IS FOR PERFECT, MY FAVORITE HUMAN BEING!

Q IS FOR QUIRKY, YOUR HUMOR IS A DELIGHT!

R IS FOR RADIANT, YOU SHINE SO BRIGHT!

S IS FOR SUPER, YOU ARE MY LITTLE HERO!

T IS FOR TALENTED, **I** KNOW YOU CAN DO IT
EVEN WHEN YOU START AT ZERO!

U IS FOR UNIQUE, YOU ARE ONE OF A KIND!

V IS FOR VALUABLE, EVERYTHING ABOUT YOU COMES TO MIND!

W IS FOR WONDERFUL, JUST ONE OF YOUR MANY QUALITIES!

XY AND Z FOR THE MILLIONS OF WORDS TO DESCRIBE HOW SPECIAL YOU ARE TO ME!

www.ingramcontent.com/pod-product-compliance
Lightning Source LLC
Chambersburg PA
CBHW042345030426
42335CB00030B/3458